The Cat Walked Through the Casserole

and other poems for children

D0961210

The Cat Walked
Through the

Carolrhoda Books, Inc.   Minneapolis

Casserole

and other poems for children

by Pamela Espeland and Marilyn Waniek
illustrated by Trina Schart Hyman,
Hilary Knight, Nancy Carlson,
and Peter E. Hanson

Thanks to Mason Williams, who inspired us with his goofy poems; and to Malcolm Andrew Watt and James Benno Nelson, who contributed questions and criticisms during the early stages of this book, when they were four.

Manufactured in the United States of America

Library of Congress Cataloging in Publication Data

Espeland, Pamela, 1951-
    The cat walked through the casserole and other poems for children.

    Summary: A collection of poems about children and their lives.
    1. Children's poetry, American. [1. American poetry] I. Waniek, Marilyn Nelson, 1946-
II. Hyman, Trina Schart, ill. III. Title.
PS3555.S54C3 1984   811'.54   84-11381
ISBN 0-87614-268-4 (lib. bdg.)

2   3   4   5   6   7   8   9   10   93   92   91   90   89   88   87   86   85

This book is for our sons, Jonah and Jacob.

THE CAT WALKED THROUGH THE CASSEROLE

The cat walked through the casserole
And tracked it on the floor
When we all rushed outside to see
The ambulance next door.
　　　So the cat had to go.

My puppy did his business
In the yard across the way
And now my dad and mom
Are sending it away
        Because the neighbor got mad.

Today my little brother
Broke Mom's best crystal vase.
It sure will be a big relief
Not to ever see HIS face
        Around here again!

IF GROWN-UPS WERE SMART

Hey, big gorilla,
Locked up in a cage!
I'm meaner than YOU were
When YOU were my age!

I eat bricks for dinner
And drink cold cement.
My mom keeps on asking
Where the house next door went.

I'm badder than you are,
And uglier, too!
If grown-ups were smart,
They'd put ME in the zoo!

IF I COULD DO WHATEVER I WANTED

If I could do whatever I wanted
Whenever I wanted to do it,
There are some things I'd go and do right now,
And some when I got around to it.

I'd send Teacher's mother a letter
With "See me soon" checked on a form.
I'd make Dad wear socks and a sweater
On days when it's sunny and warm.

I'd drill the dentist's molars.
I'd cut the barber's hair.
I'd make my mom take baths all the time
And not let her go anywhere.

I'd give the principal spankings.
I'd yell at the sitter a lot.
I'd make all the farmers eat spinach –
And I'd give the doctor a shot!

MARY ANN THE WITCH GIRL

Mary Ann the witch girl
Sneaks out at night
Closes the screen door
Locks it up tight
Faces the apple tree
Turns toward the house
Whispers a magic spell
Squeaks like a mouse
Chooses a special star
Then makes two wishes...

And passes arithmetic
And NEVER does dishes!

BLUE TATTOO

My uncle has a blue tattoo
Right there on his belly.
I think it's wonderful,
But Aunt Jean thinks it's silly.

My cousin Shelley broke her arm
And got to wear a cast,
And then she got to wear the names
Of everyone in class.

My brother got a tooth knocked out
And now his new one's plastic.
Our mother thinks it's horrible,
But I think it's fantastic!

Everywhere I look around,
Everyone I see,
Everyone else is different,
Everyone else is interesting,
Everyone else is lucky,
Everyone but me!

FATHER FITZGERALD

Father Fitzgerald says we all have souls,
But I don't know what souls are all about.
What IS a soul? That's what I want to know.
And how did mine get in? Can it get out?

Is it like a stomach, or a heart?
Does it float inside me like a tiny cloud?
When I cry, or lie, or forget to say my prayers,
Does it squinch its eyes up tight and groan out loud?

Father Fitzgerald says I shouldn't sin
So my soul will still be pure after I grow up.
But what I want to know is, can I lose it?
Like if I get the flu sometime and throw up?

NOSE-PICKERS

Look at them nose-pickers!
Ain't they gross?
Stickin' they fingers
Up they nose!

Look at them nose-pickers!
Ain't they dumb?
Some use a pointer.
Some use a thumb.

Look at them nose-pickers!
Ain't they obscene?
Everyone's a nose-picker –
Know what I mean?

GRANDPA'S WHISKERS

My grandpa came last Saturday
To visit for a week.
I kind of liked his looks at first –
Then he rubbed my face with his cheek.

His cheek is all covered with whiskers.
He's scraped all the skin off my nose.
He's tickled me so much, I'm WRINKLED!
I'll sure be relieved when he goes!

THOMAS HAS A GIRLFRIEND

Thomas has a girlfriend.
Her name is Emmy Lou.
She knows about biology
And she plays baseball, too.

She taught him how to broad jump.
She taught him to play chess.
Sometimes they lie and watch the clouds,
And those times are the best.

Thomas has a girlfriend.
Her name is Emmy Lou.
If you knew someone like her,
You'd want a girlfriend, too.

ALONE

I used to hate

    to be left alone.

Now I love

    to be left alone.

I used to cry

    when I was left alone.

Now sometimes I try

    to be left alone.

I used to scream

    when I was left alone.

Now I dream

    when I'm left alone.

Now I feel free

    when I'm left alone.

I can be me

    when I'm left alone.

LUCK

I didn't come out of my mother.
I don't have my father's green eyes.
No one in the family looks like me.
People are always surprised.

I think we're a happier family
Than if we were all kings and queens.
We're so lucky we all found each other.
That's what being adopted means.

DAFFODILS

What kind of flower will I become
After I die someday?
Grandmother turned into daffodils
Last year when she went away.

I was awfully sad when she left us.
I miss all the stories she told.
Her lap was as soft as a pillow.
I wonder why people get old.

Mom says that Gram went to live with God
Up where the sky is blue.
Dad says she's sleeping inside the earth,
But I know that this isn't true.

Grandmother turned into daffodils.
They're blooming all over her grave.
Whenever we visit on Saturdays,
As soon as they see me, they wave.

JAMES MADE HIMSELF INVISIBLE

James made himself invisible.
We told him not to do it.
But when Mom shut his bedroom door,
Our brother James walked through it.

He went into the kitchen, where
That silly little kid
Climbed up to get the cookie jar
And slipped and dropped the lid.

Our father jumped out of his chair
And yelled, "What's that I hear?"
Then Mom tripped over James's foot
And screamed into his ear.

His eyes showed up, and then his nose.
Our parents were so shocked
That Dad said, "James, you'll go to bed
ALL WEEK at six o'clock!"

When James came crying back to us,
We said, "We told you so!
When kids become invisible,
They can't let grown-ups know!"

NO FAIR

Why don't I get to stay out playing late?
Everyone else is still there.
They're still playing stickball and hopscotch and stuff –
My mommy and daddy aren't fair!

It's not even dark! I'm not tired at all!
So why do I have to come in?
Why can't I stay out just four minutes more?
The fun's just begun to begin!

I USED TO HAVE A DINOSAUR

I used to have a dinosaur.
I fed it from my plate.
For years I fed my dinosaur
The things I never ate,
Like liver, squash, and succotash,
Oatmeal and pickled beets,
Cottage cheese, and runny eggs –
The things that NO ONE eats!

WHEN I GROW UP

When I grow up
I'll grow a beard,
I'll never wash between my toes,

And when I eat
In a restaurant
And feel like it, I'll blow my nose.

I won't take baths
Or do my math.
I'll eat whatever I want to eat.

I'll drive a big car
With a convertible top
And make Dad sit in the back seat!

LOOK AGAIN

Daddy looked inside the closet.
Then he shut the window, too.
Then he looked behind my dresser.
Then he looked inside my shoe.
Then he looked beneath my mattress.
Then he left and closed the door.

But how do I KNOW there's nothing there?
How do I know for SURE?

QUEEN OF THE RAINBOW

I used to be Queen of the Rainbow.
I wasn't always just me.
I used to wear clothes made of roses.
I used to be fearless and free.
I used to have planets for playmates
And whole constellations for friends.
I talked every day to the sunshine.
I danced every night with the wind.
I used to be pretty and graceful.
I used to do everything right.
I used to be brave as the thunder
And not scared of noises at night.
I used to live high in the heavens.
I came down to earth with a sigh.

I used to be Queen of the Rainbow.
I used to be Queen of the Sky.

HISTORY

In school we're learning all about the Pilgrims –
The clothes they wore, and what Thanksgiving means.
I like to learn about the things that they did,
But they missed out on lots of things I've seen.

I'd like to show a Pilgrim kid a jet plane,
And how to call a friend up on the phone,
And what a TV is, and running water,
And how I turn on lights when I'm alone.

Maybe someday some future kid will study
The things that people did in history.
She'll look into her very own computer –
And the picture looking back will be of me!

HAND-SHADOWS

The apartment gets all cozy
When our mom comes home at night.
We help her take her shoes off,
Then we turn out all the lights.

Annie-Sue brings out the candle,
Walter Junior lights a match,
And Maydeen puts on a record –
Then we all sit back to watch.

Mother says, "Fetch me my glasses –
Do you want the wolf and all?"
Then she tells a long, long story
With hand-shadows on the wall.

Illustration Credits